Kerfed Linings Made Easy
An Illustrated Guide

Dale Henry Brown

DEDICATION

To my incredible wife of 53 years, Jan, and my amazing children and spouses, Tim (Christel), Tami (Gordon), Jeremy (Shea), Dale II (Lindsay), who have always admired and supported me in my woodworking, spurring me on to hone the skills of my craft.

CONTENTS

KERFED LININGS

INTRODUCTION

For me, woodworking is a passion. Not my only passion, or even the thing I am most passionate about, but it is a passion. Specifically, making ukuleles. I suppose it all started when I was about ten years old. One day my dad brought home a little ukulele, and I fell in love with it. It led to a love for acoustic instruments. To me, there is no sound in the world, like music played on acoustic instruments.

Over the years, I have built many ukuleles and guitars, utilizing various techniques and resources. I have built kits and from scratch, mostly from scratch. The ones from scratch provide the greatest satisfaction. I have even made instruments from trees that have been cut down in the neighborhood.

There are many resources available for luthiers these days. When it comes to ukuleles, you can buy precut sides and backs which require shaping and thinning, necks, fingerboards (blank or shaped with fret slots), bindings, headpiece laminates, and kerfed linings. You can even buy complete ready to build kits. But true satisfaction comes from crafting from scratch.

The topic of this book is kerfed linings. You can purchase these relatively inexpensively from resources such as StewMac, which I have done over the years. The reason is that making your own kerfed linings is not an easy task, and it is time-consuming. It's not easy because you are dealing with a relatively small piece of wood in which you have to cut slots to make flexible enough to attach to the curved sides of the ukulele or guitar. I struggled to make these and was never happy with the results until I discovered and developed a technique which is not only very efficient but enjoyable as well.

My desire is that this little guide will enable you to reach the level of satisfaction that comes from making everything from scratch, even the kerfed linings. So, let's get started!

See a demo video of the Kerfed Lining jig
in action on YouTube at:
https://youtu.be/ezqpNNk5pTI
also at
dhbinspire.com
where you will find more books by
Dale Henry Brown

SELECTING THE WOOD

Before we begin our discussion on selecting wood for kerfed linings, I should mention that there are different styles of linings used in instrument making. Those styles include kerfed, reversed, solid, and tentallone linings. There are some wonderful articles on the Internet explaining each of these from a historical and usage context. If this is of interest to you a little time spent searching on the Internet will yield plenty of information. For this book, we will be dealing with kerfed linings.

Various types of wood are used in making kerfed linings. The most common woods used are basswood and mahogany. The important characteristic of these woods is that they are lightweight and do not add significant weight to the project. Other woods may also be used. You could use just about any kind of wood if it can be cut and shaped properly.

CUTTING OUT THE KERFING STRIPS

Cutting the wood down to the necessary size involves using a table saw or a bandsaw to cut the wood into strips. For a guitar, the strips need to be 1/4-inch by 5/8-inch. For a ukulele, they are 1/4-inch by 3/8-inch.

The following is my procedure.

STEP ONE

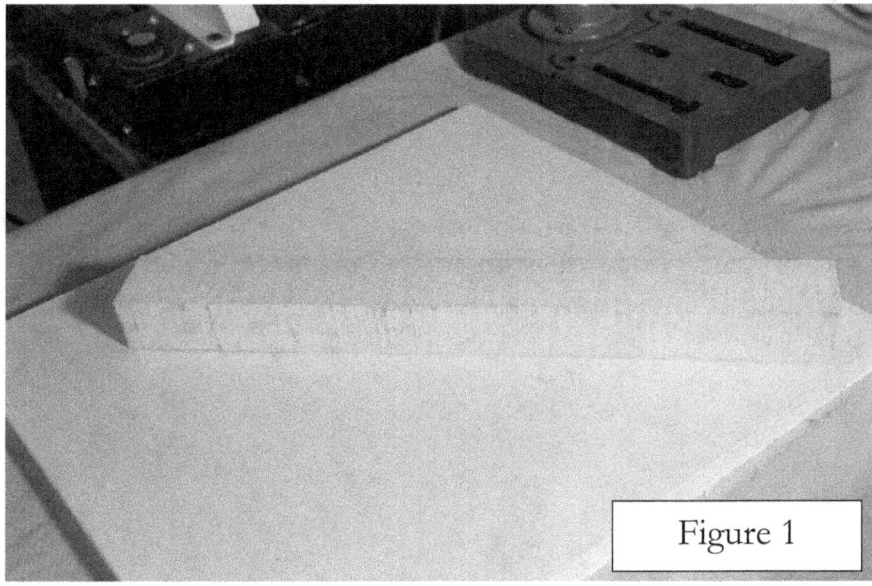

Figure 1

Select your wood. Figure 1 shows a 2-inch square block of basswood I am using for illustration in this text. As previously stated, you can use different kinds of woods, even scrap wood you have lying around. But it needs to be cut to the exact measurements.

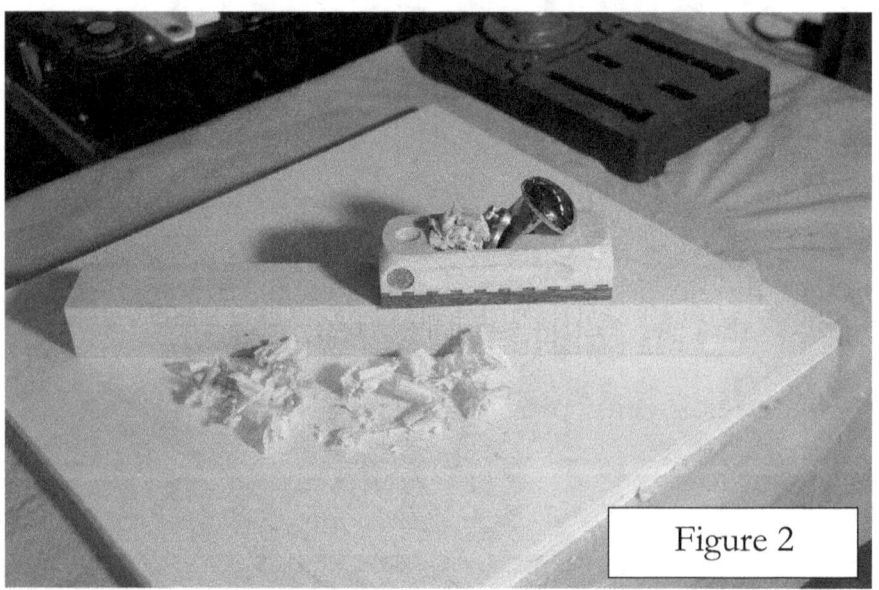

Figure 2

STEP TWO

Since this block of wood is rough on all four sides, I will need to plane one side (Figure 2). This is the side that will go against the fence when I cut it on the table saw. A power planer or drum sander may also be used for this task.

STEP THREE

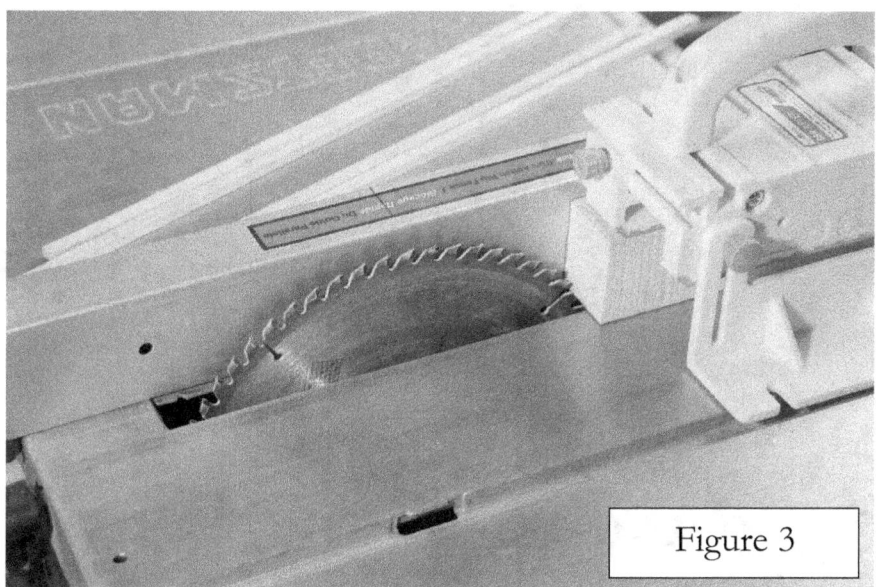

Figure 3

It is now time to make my first cut. Since I'm going to be cutting a narrow piece of wood with a blade that is over 2 inches high, I must be extremely careful. In Figure 3, you see a device that is holding the wood in place. It is called a Grr-Ripper. There are inventions that are nice, but this one is fantastic. I would encourage you to check it out by going to their website. Just Google Grr-Ripper. (This is not a paid advertisement. I just happen to love this product!)

In this step, I am cutting a slab of wood 1/4-inch thick. That is a pretty narrow cut and made much easier with the Grr-ripper.

Since this block of wood is 2 inches square, I can cut several slabs which will yield a good number of kerfed linings.

STEP FOUR

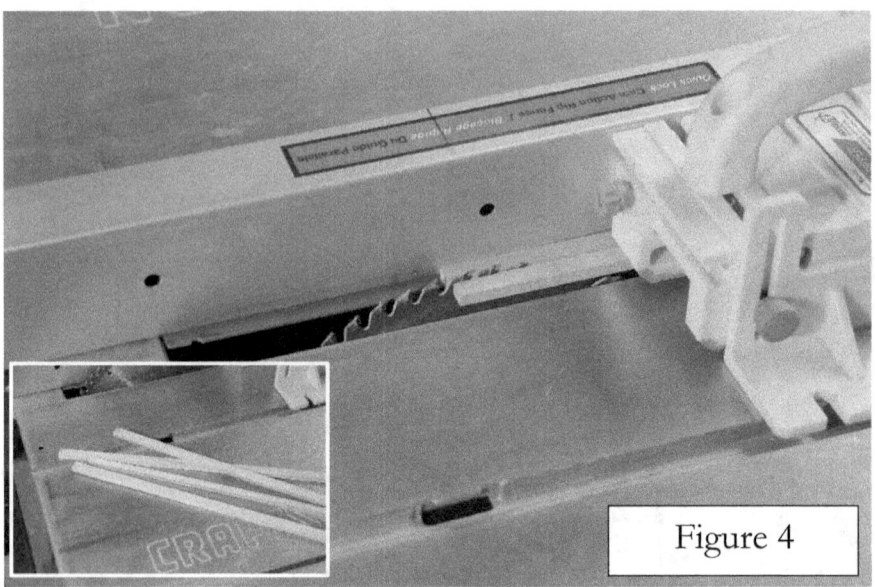

Figure 4

With the slabs cut from the block, a final cut of 3/8-inch can now be made that will yield our basic linings strip. If you are making kerfed linings for a guitar, you will want to make these cuts 5/8-inch.

We have now completed the creation of our basic kerfed linings and are about to embark upon the most fun and enjoyable part of making kerfed linings – building and using a couple of jigs to shape the linings and cut the slots. I promise you it will be a rewarding journey.

CONSTRUCTING THE SHAPING JIG

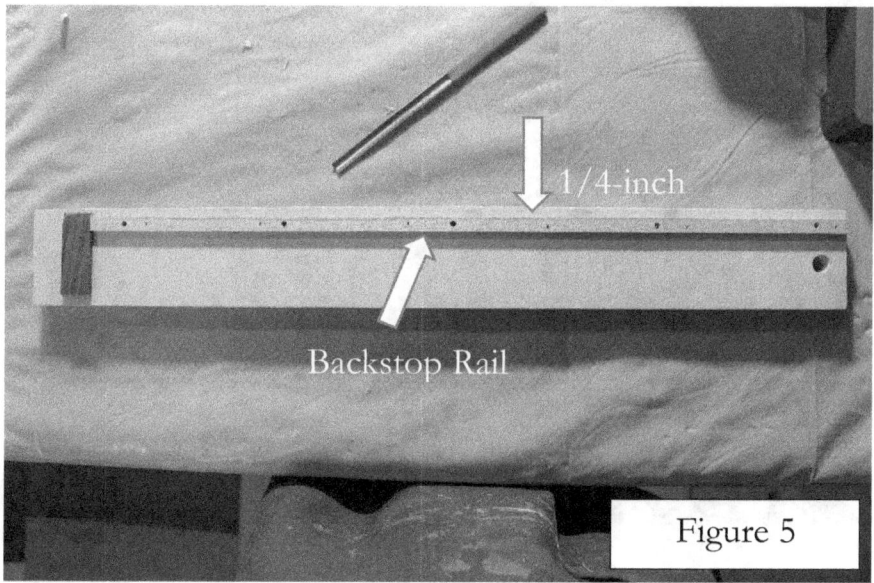

Figure 5

Figure 5 shows the jig made for planing the kerfed linings. The hole on the right side in the middle is simply there for hanging on a nail when not in use. Most of the jigs I use in instrument making are hanging on nails from a beam in my shop.

The jig is 2 feet long and 3 inches wide. These dimensions are somewhat arbitrary but are what I came up with to be able to handle any length of kerfing I will be making.

The lower arrow is pointing to what I call the backstop rail against which the kerfed lining rests while it is being planed. It is 22 inches long, 1/2-inch-wide, and 1/4-inch in height. It is inset 1/4-inch.

The base piece is made from plywood, and the backstop rail is made from curly maple. Again, other kinds of wood will work, even MDF.

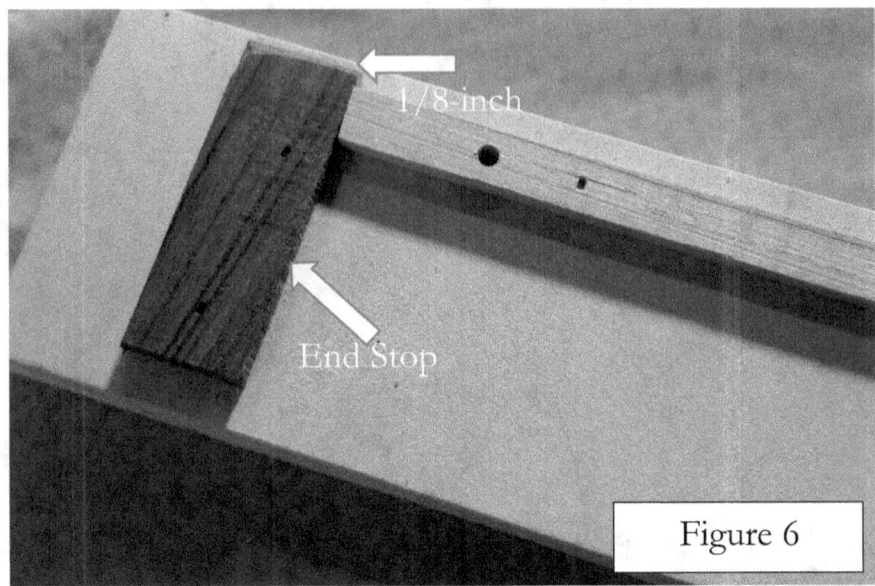

Figure 6

Figure 6 shows the end of the jig with a stop made from a piece of scrap rosewood. Its dimensions are 2 3/8 inches by 7/8-inch. It is important to note two things about this end stop.

First, it should be slightly lower in height than the backstop rail.

Figure 6a

Second, it should be recessed slightly from the edge of the board the lining rests on so that it does not interfere with the planing action.

Now, let's put this jig to work!

USING THE SHAPING JIG

Figure 7

The shaping process begins by placing one of the lining strips prepared earlier against the backstop rail butted up against the stop. The 1/4-inch edge rests against the backstop rail. A little more stability can be attained by using some double-sided tape to hold the strip in place.

Shaping the strip to make the kerfed lining is a simple matter of planing the strip at an angle to create the triangle shape shown in the inset picture of Figure 7.

A quality, sharp block plane is necessary for this process. Set the blade so that the plane moves smoothly along the wood peeling off small shavings without stuttering. With a little practice when done properly, this process is very gratifying.

CONSTRUCTING THE KERFED LINING JIG

Before we begin illustrating the construction of the kerfed lining jig, I want to give credit where credit is due. The original idea for this jig came from a picture I saw on Pinterest. A little digging and I found that it appeared on the website of Fine Woodworking. The total amount of information on this jig is what you see in the picture. My research yielded no further explanation on details of the construction. There was one reference in a blog of someone inquiring about details of construction, but no such explanation followed. The contribution of the unnamed designer is greatly appreciated.

If you search the Internet for kerfed lining jigs, you will find a plethora of information and designs of all kinds. There are professionally designed high-tech systems used in mass production, and there are automated designs made by individuals that are quite impressive. But I found this simple little design to be ingenious and fitting my style of handcrafting ukuleles and guitars.

What follows is a detailed description of how I constructed this jig from the picture in the article in Fine Woodworking. I have applied my expression in building the jig as I expect the reader will do in constructing their version.

I would suggest that you view my YouTube video showing the jig in action. This will give you a context for what you are about to read. https://youtu.be/ezqpNNk5pTI

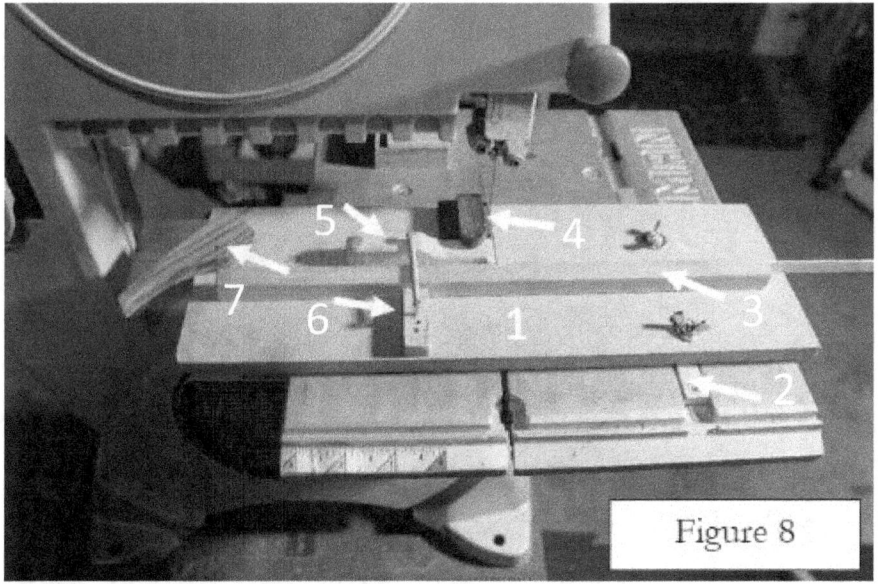

Figure 8

The parts of this kerfed lining jig are as follows:

1 – Base
2 – Miter Guide
3 – Rail
4 – Rocker Arm
5 – Rocker Arm Guide
6 – Spring Tension Block
7 – Exit Guide

Other miscellaneous parts include screws, washers and nuts, a pin for the rocker arm, a spring, and the miter guide. Each one of these will be explained as we get to the part in the construction where they are employed.

Don't be overwhelmed by all the parts; we will explain them step-by-step so you should have no difficulty in building your own kerfed lining jig.

Base

Since it is important for the base to be perfectly flat, MDF fits the bill best. The base is 14 inches long and 5 inches wide cut from 1/2-inch MDF.

Miter Guide

The miter guide needs to be attached first because everything else is relevant to its position on the base. If you are experienced in woodworking, you know that miter guides come in a couple of different styles, shown below.

Figure 9

Figure 10

Figure 9 shows the guide sleeve with little flanges under which a portion of the rail must slide, while figure 10 is just an open sleeve. The different miter guides are not interchangeable. My Craftsman bandsaw that I use for this project has the flanges, and I use an old guide mounted on the base. If your bandsaw has the open guide sleeve, you can use a piece of hardwood as your miter guide. If you have the flanged type of miter guide, you could still construct a guide out of wood if you have the skills and patience to do so.

Whichever type you use it must be mounted square on the base board in a location that places the bandsaw blade at the center of the base board (refer to figure 8). Make sure that any screws you use to mount the miter guide are recessed, so they do not drag when sliding.

Rail

The jig in our illustration is set up for making the kerfed linings for ukuleles, or mandolins, so the specs are a little different if you are doing guitar construction. The rail in our illustration is 13 inches long and 1/2-inch square. For guitar construction the kerfed linings are 5/8-inch by 1/4-inch, so the rail should be slightly higher than 5/8 inch so that the spring will clear the top of it. In this case, the rail could be 11/16-inch x 1/2-inch. It is located 2 5/8-inches from the back edge of the base.

The rail is secured with screws through the bottom. Again, make sure they are recessed, so they do not drag on the tabletop. Before inserting the screws, I secured the rail with some super glue making it easier to attach the screws.

Rocker Arm

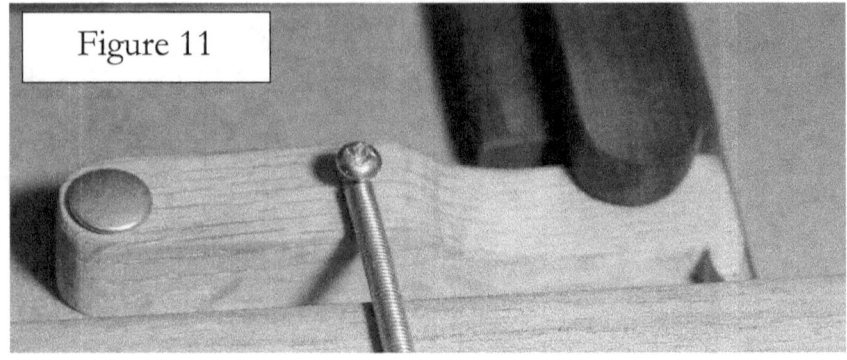

Figure 11

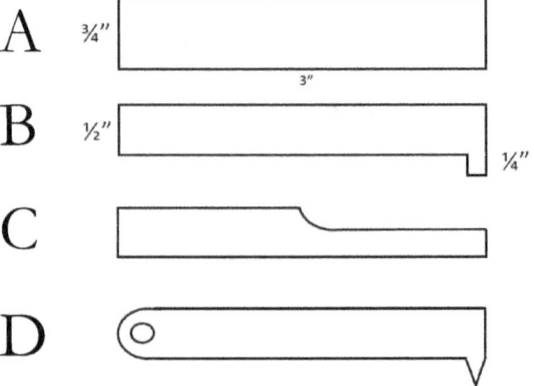

A   ¾"

B   ½"   ¼"

C

D

Figure 12

The Rocker Arm is made from a piece of oak 3 1/2 inches long, 3/4-inch-wide and 1/2-inch high. Figure 12 illustrates how to cut and shape the rocker arm. Begin by cutting 1/4-inch from the original block (A) leaving 1/4-inch at one end, as illustrated (B).

From the top of the block, beginning about halfway, shape it down to 1/4-inch (C). I used my bandsaw for the initial cut and then my spindle sander to shape the curved line.

The little quarter-inch nubbin seen in B of Figure 12 is now shaped to a point as seen in figure D. The purpose of this point is that it will drop into the slot that has been previously cut to set the jig to the exact distance for the next cut.

Finally, on the Rocker Arm, drill a 1/4-inch hole as shown in step D. Lay the Rocker Arm aside for later assembly.

IMPORTANT NOTE

Before continuing our project, it will be necessary to make the cut with the bandsaw into the base. Since you already have the miter guide installed simply put it on the bandsaw, turn it on and run the blade up to the rail. This will establish a reference point for the rest of the assembly.

Rocker Arm Guide

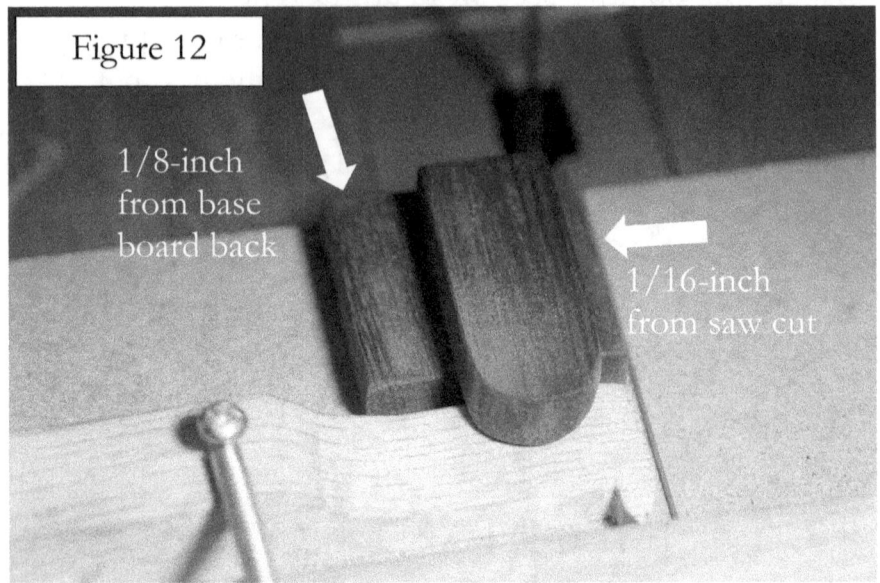

Figure 12

1/8-inch
from base
board back

1/16-inch
from saw cut

The Rocker Arm Guide adds a little extra control to the Rocker Arm. It is made of rosewood and consists of two pieces. The base piece is 1 1/4-inches square and 1/4-inch thick. The top piece with the rounded end is 1 5/8-inches by 5/8-inch and 1/4-inch thick.

Round the top piece and sand it and its base.

With the saw groove cut, we can now install the Rocker Arm Guide. On this jig, I simply super glued them on. Screws may be added if desired.

The base of the Rocker Arm Guide is positioned 1/16-inch from the saw groove and 1/8-inch from the back.

The top piece hangs over the edge of the base 5/8-inch.

Assembling the Rocker Arm

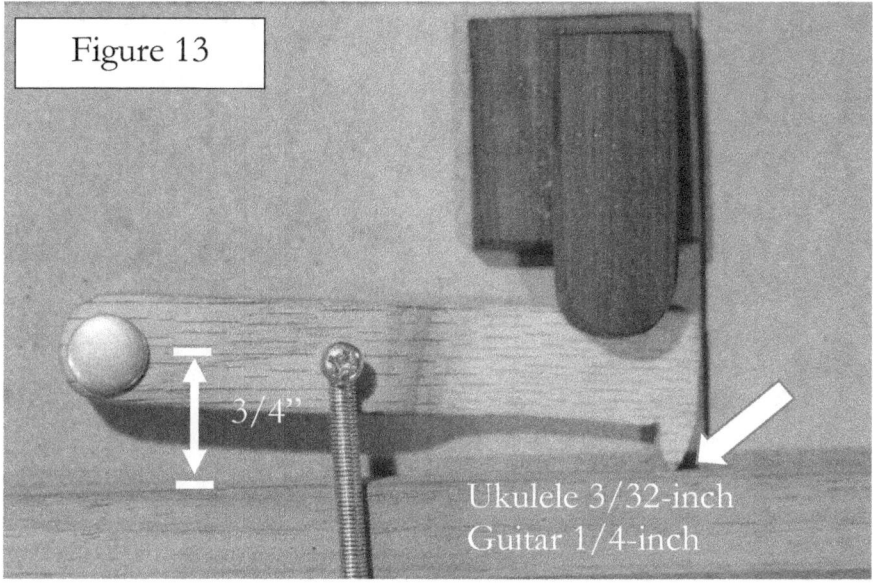

Figure 13

3/4"

Ukulele 3/32-inch
Guitar 1/4-inch

The center of the Rocker Arm rests 3/4-inch from the rail. The head with the point on it is positioned to be the distance you want between the grooves in the kerfed linings and the saw blade.

Rocker Arm Pin

Once the position is established for the Rocker Arm, mark and drill the hole for the pin on which the Rocker Arm will rotate.

Now let's take a look at the pin. In the original drawing shown on the Fine Woodworking website, it looks like a nail was used for the pin. At our local Manard's store, I found a beautiful aluminum pin that worked perfectly and added a little more class to the project. They most likely can also be found at Home Depot or Lowe's.

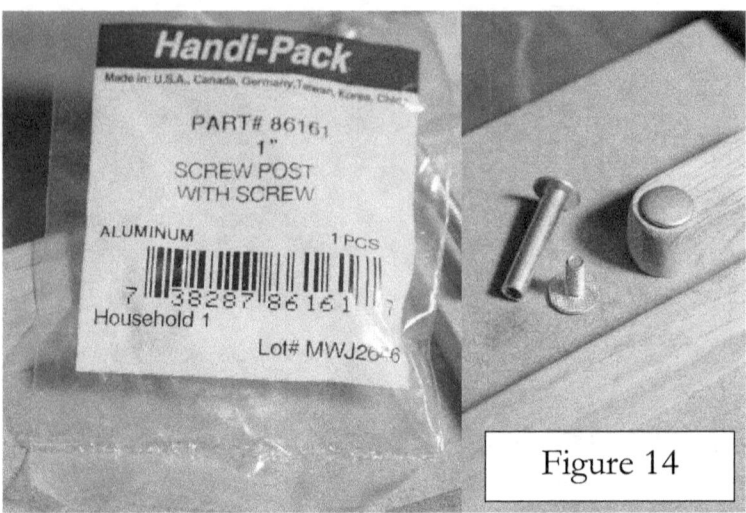

Figure 14

If you choose to use a nail or something else for the pin, you will need to consider the size of the hole you drill.

Spring Tension Block

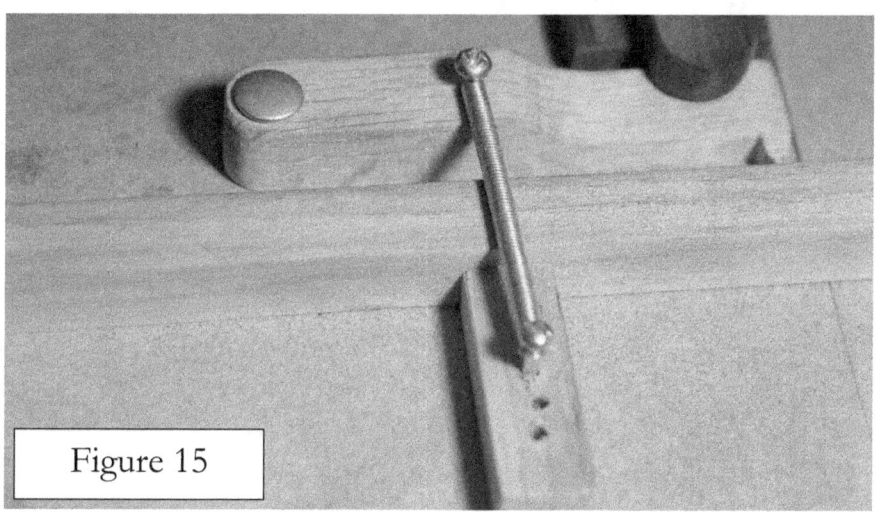

Figure 15

Figure 15 shows the spring and the spring tension block. The block is 1/2-inch wide, 1 5/8 inches long, and 3/8-inch high. The three holes that are drilled into the top (albeit not very precisely) are there to apply different tensions. Place the block, as shown in Figure 15, at the halfway point of the Rocker Arm.

The spring was purchased from our local Manard's store to replace the rubber band that is shown in the Fine Woodworking website article. After experimenting with a couple of different springs, I was satisfied with the action this spring provides. If you would guess by looking at the picture that it is about 2 inches long, you would be correct. Use a couple of appropriate screws to mount the spring as shown.

We are almost finished! There is one more very important part that must be in place to protect our kerfed lining as it exits the jig.

Exit Guide

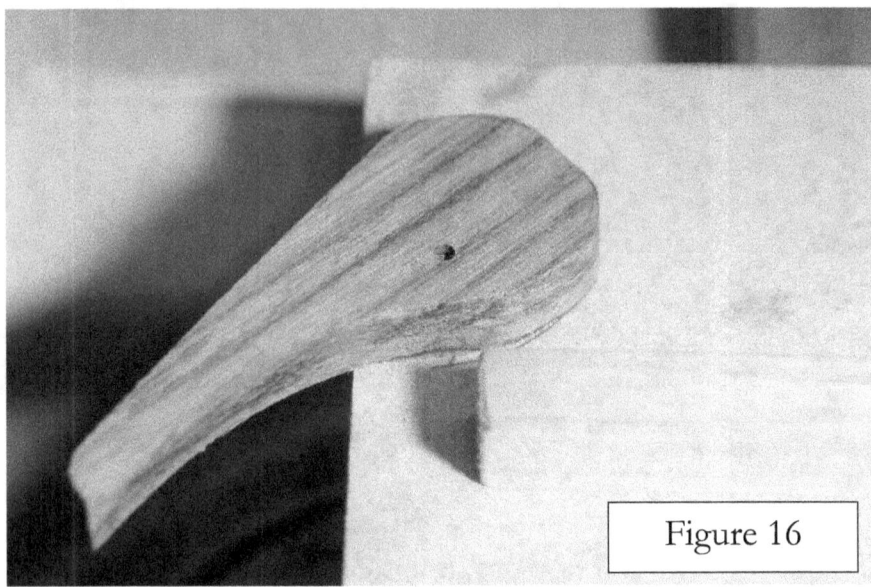

Figure 16

As I lookd at Figure 16, I thought perhaps I should have called it the "duck."

At first glance, you might wonder what purpose that funny-looking little device serves. If you watched the YouTube video, then you know that it serves to guide the kerfed lining away from the housing of the bandsaw as it exits the jig. You need to use your imagination as to how you will design it, but it needs to be designed so that the kerfing easily slides away from the bandsaw.

Setup

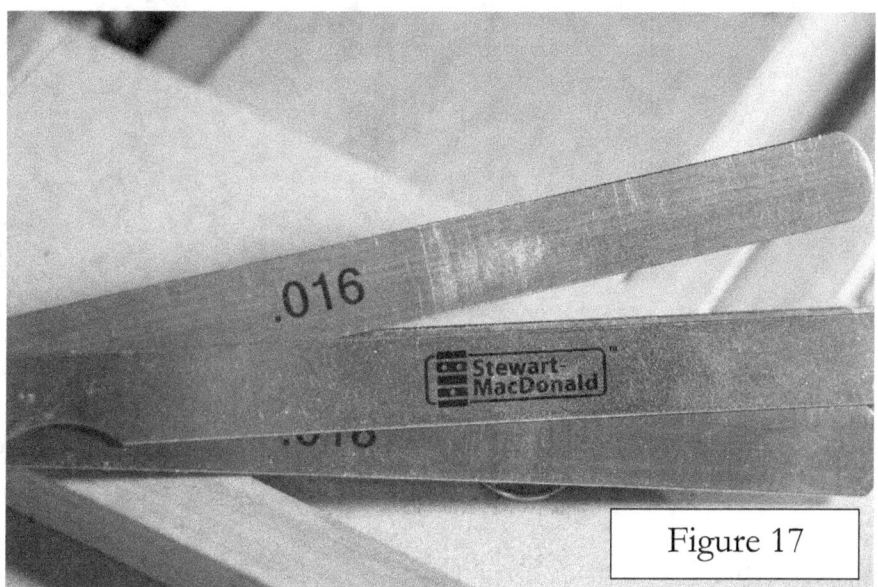

Figure 17

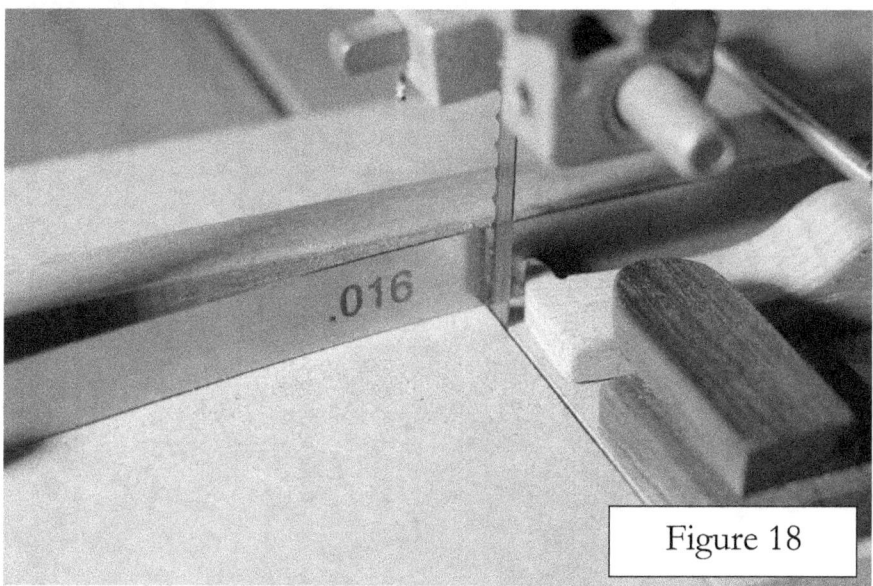

Figure 18

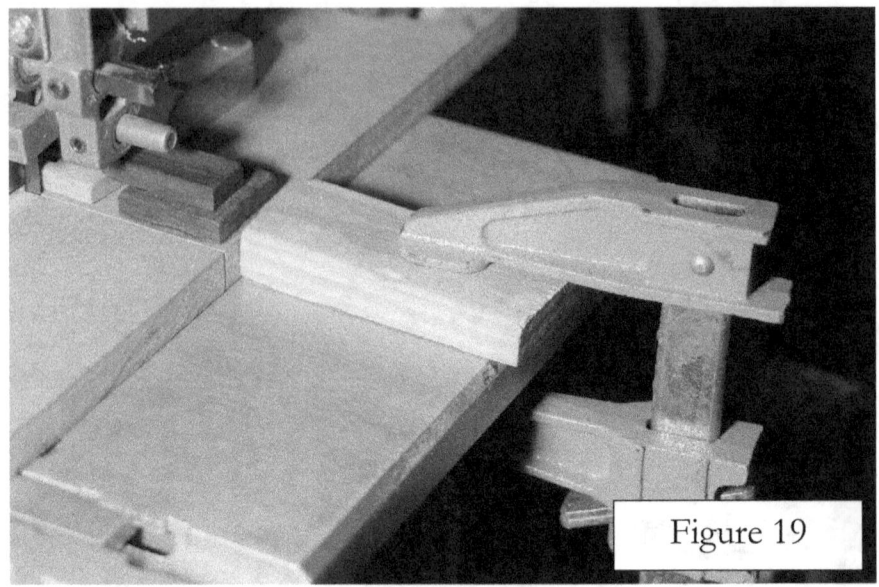

Figure 19

The set up for the jig is relatively simple. You will need the following:

a feeler gauge

a block of wood

a clamp

Referring to Figures 17 - 19, first, place the feeler gauge (.016 works great) against the rail and slide the jig until it gently contacts the bandsaw blade. Place a block of wood against the backside of the jig and clamp it down. You're all set to cut some great kerfed linings.

Operating the Jig

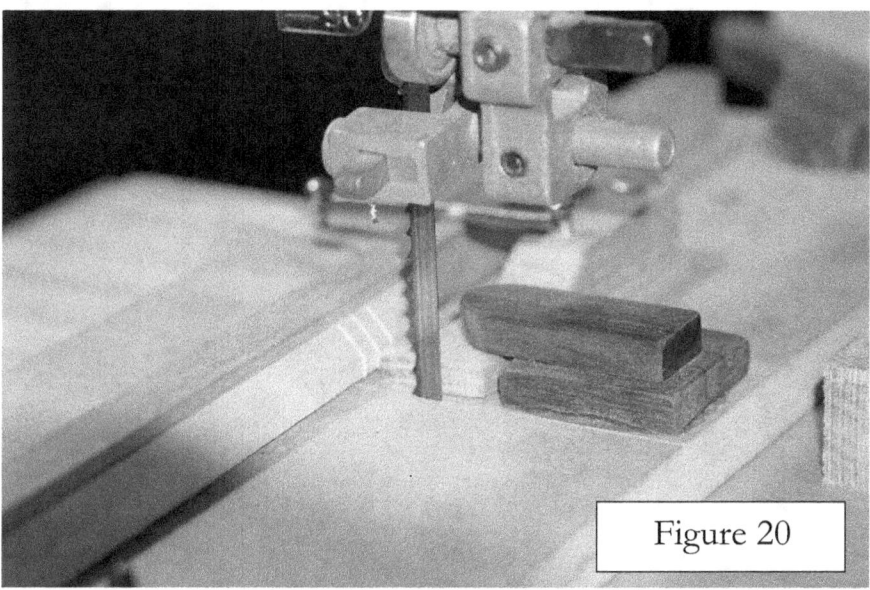

Figure 20

Placing a kerfing strip into the jig, make a cut, then use your finger to open the Rocker Arm just enough to let you slide the lining until the point on the Rocker Arm rests in the just cut groove. Your next cut will be perfectly spaced. Keep doing this until the entire strip is cut.

Note: I would recommend leaving about a half-inch or so of material at each end of the kerfed lining.

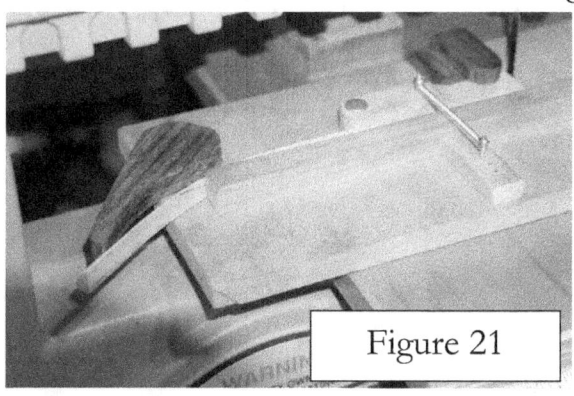

Figure 21

Keep an eye on the exit point and give a little assistance if needed to keep the lining moving freely.